The Rise and Fall of Tides

Poems and Photographs

Copyright © 2024 by Curtis J. Badger

All rights reserved.

ISBN 978-1-62806-427-8 (print | paperback)
ISBN 978-1-62806-428-5 (print | hardback)

Library of Congress Control Number 2024919599

Published by Salt Water Media
29 Broad Street, Suite 104
Berlin, MD 21811
www.saltwatermedia.com

On the cover: The headwaters of the Machipongo River at Piggin Road
Cover photograph and interior photographs by Curtis J. Badger
with the exception of the older family photos. Those photographers are unknown.

The Rise and Fall of Tides

Poems and Photographs

Curtis J. Badger

Contents

Introduction 9

The Rise and Fall of Tides

Joynes Neck Gives Birth to Folly Creek 13

The Rise and Fall of Tides 15

The Edge 17

Marsh Henning Tides 19

Subtlety and Stridency 21

Walking on Cheese 22

On the Pocomoke 23

Hummocks 25

Thin Water Glide 27

Sunrise and Ocean 29

Foodways

Clamming 33

Spot and Pigfish 34

Salted Fish 35

Fish of the Day 36

Cock-a-leekie Soup 37

Life on the Halfshell 38

Bessie Gunter 39

Clam Chowder 41

Love Dumplings 42

Grandma's Hog's Jole 43

The Women All Singing 45

Digging Potatoes 47

Apple Pie 48

Closer to Home

The Birth of the Day 50

The Cat 51

Brant 53

Jimmy King 54

Contents

Clinging to the Bough 55

MRI 57

The Cat, 2 58

Radio People 59

The Cat and the Clock 60

Spoiling the Cat 61

The Concrete Fleet 63

Fatwood Fire Starter 64

Honeysuckle Always Climbs Clockwise 65

Wisteria 66

Gifts of Time and Place 67

Lake Floyd 69

The Ebb and Flood of Birds 71

Too Late to Die Young 72

Passion, Not Money 73

1/250 at f/8 74

The Day the Old Hotel Burned 75

Family Matters

Red Bank Place 78

Captain John 79

Genetic Navigation 81

Aunt Easter 83

I Am Not the Child You Lost 84

Some Wounds Do Not Bleed 85

A Christmas Story 86

The Red Tricycle 89

Introduction

I began writing poems relatively late in life. I began this collection in January 2024 when I was 78, and finished it five months later, at the end of May. I was inspired by an old friend from high school, Buck Boggs, who in 2023 published two volumes of poetry. I was greatly impressed by Buck's ability to capture a wide range of feeling and emotion with a minimum of words. Having written a lot of highly detailed non-fiction in my working life, I do not share Buck's gift of minimalism, try as I might.

Most of the poems in this collection have been simmering somewhere in my subconscious for a decade, probably longer. It turns out that poetry was the tool I needed to mine them, to extract them and expose them to the light of day. Poetry is the language of freedom; it goes where narrative dare not tread. It allows aspiration of that which has lain dormant.

Most of the poems here are about two things very important to me: family and landscape. The two are inseparable. My family has lived on the Eastern Shore of Virginia since the mid-17th century, planters and mariners who likely came from the Essex coast in England and found a home among the islands and bays of the Virginia coast. We have lived closely with the land and the sea. We nurtured the land and the land nurtured us.

Most of the poems are factual, especially those dealing with family and landscape. Some relate events that actually happened, and some begin there and veer off into events that might have happened.

I have had a passion for photography all my life, especially black and white photography, and it seemed a natural marriage to join poems and photographs in this book. Black and white photographs seem to me a visual form of poetry. By removing color, you are reducing the image to its essence. And so it is with poetry. The challenge is to create an image not by adding words, but by subtracting them, mining a thought to get at its core.

This collection is dedicated to people I love very much, my wife Lynn, our son Tom, and our daughter-in-law Scarlett. And it is dedicated to our family – past, present, and future. A family history is a journey through time, and like most journeys, there are days of easy travel followed by periods of darkness and times of loss. But it all eventually comes together and is weaved into a familial fabric, a patchwork of generations that blurs the context of the times.

The Rise and Fall of Tides

Joynes Neck Gives Birth to Folly Creek

Folly Creek was born in seams of crooked soil
in a dark and private place on Joynes Neck.

Folly Creek was mothered by a hidden spring
covered by the rotting leaves of oak and gum.

Folly Creek was fathered by a swollen mass
a passing nimbus casting itself upon the private place.

If you want to taste the birth of a creek
you are sucking on the marrow bone in here
in this quiet and fertile seep
the spring thrusting its way through dark soil
pulled by earth's gravity in its moment of birth
and then,
in its maturity,
the rhythm of earth and moon
together
push and pull
the rise and fall of tides.

The Rise and Fall of Tides

Perhaps it is a matter of religion,
the rise and fall of tides.

Faith is required
when you stake your claim and break ground
marking land as your own
just beyond the capricious limits of ebb and flood.
You must believe in the power that controls the flow,
the rise and fall,
the twice daily advance and retreat of tides.

Perhaps the natives had it right.
They settled on high land and visited the coast
for fish during the warm season
and birds and animals in winter.
Did the natives lack faith,
or did they have no use for ebb and flood,
the rise and fall?

The English settled in the necks of land
between the waters,
which were their highways
their links with the land they left,
the homes they might one day return to.
They needed that option.

The natives had no need for deep water.
They were already at home,
settled near shallow headwaters
where duck potato and arum grew.
They harvested wild rice
wove baskets from grasses
collected shells and made beads
to trade for stone tools and other treasures.
They traveled by footpath and had no need for oceans.
They had no need for faith.

Captain Tom settled on Red Bank Creek
east of Hog Island Bay
and he built a home, cleared land, grew crops
and the creek and the bay were his footpath
his avenue of commerce.

But when the railroad came in 1884
he bought sixty acres due west of the station,
built a house with a big porch facing east.
He could sit in his rocker
and watch the trains come and go all day.

Did Captain Tom lose faith in the ebb and flood?
Was he tired of shadow-boxing northeasters?
Or did he become like the natives,
knowing at last where home was
and in need of faith no more?

The Edge

I stepped from the boat
and found no bottom
only the cold pull of the tide
pulling me into the edge
into the dark edge
the chasm that separates the known from the unknown.

I must have been ten
stepping from my father's skiff
onto this edge
entering something undefinable
the cold persistence of the ocean
the crash and roar
the hiss of retreat.

I was at the edge of the world
but I knew there was more.
The land had its limits
defined by the longest lick of low tide
but the ocean was rife and verdant
the ocean was the avenue, the future, the world without end.

On this edge, this precarious edge
where one world ends and another begins
is where I want to be,
to live in this dark violent edge
where land and sea collide.

Then I can concentrate on the real issues
ebb and flood
the hope of the horizon
the power of the sea
great energy that comes from no discernable source.

Standing alone at the edge of the sea,
I am close to something I cannot comprehend,
beginning to get my feet wet....

Marsh Henning Tides

I killed my first bird at thirteen
a marsh hen
clapper rail by name
with my father in a cedar skiff
a storm offshore and a flooding tide
covering the islands and marshes
until the swelling landscape disappeared
and all was water
only a few green tufts between ocean and fastland
and in them hid the marsh hens
abandoned by nature
made vulnerable by the reluctance of the tide to fall.

It's time my father said.
I rolled the shells around in my pocket
they clicked together warmly
I loaded both barrels of the double
and when my father nudged the skiff into a green tump,
the bird rose against the wind and hung like a wet washcloth.

The shot seemed unnatural in this quiet flooded place,
an ellipse of foam appeared on the water
and in the ellipse the marsh hen lay broken,
one wing flapping, flying
in a final act of muscle memory.
I raised the gun to shoot again
and I felt my father's hand upon my shoulder.
I lay the gun down.
It's a good tide, he said.

Two hours passed and the marsh was green again
grasses reclaimed the landscape,
swollen bays and creeks gone slack,
waterways defined once more.
I sat on the wooden seat in the skiff
a dozen birds at my feet
water pooled around them
around me
as though a baptism had taken place,
a christening of sorts
in a flooded marsh
with a coastal storm
bringing something memorable from the sea.

Subtlety and Stridency

I have nothing against mountains
but I prefer my feet firmly planted in sand
or in fibrous, thick mud where clams grow.
I prefer salt in the air I breathe.

Mountains are too strident
geology flexing its muscles.
I prefer subtlety to stridency,
the remains of mountains
fragments weathered smooth
and moved by millennia of rains,
washing the mountains to the sea.

Walking on Cheese

Today I walk on cheese.
The high marsh on Bellevue Farm
is like a thousand-acre wedge
of muddy Swiss
perforated by the tunnels and dens
of legions of fiddler crabs
that scurry along the banks
waving their singular
oversized claw
like some awkward weapon,
intent on defending
this tenuous territory,
not marsh and not land
but something of both.
The footing is firm
like a dry sponge
thirsty for water
it shivers as I shift my weight.
Here on this land of cheese
grow plants that are
neither upland nor wetland,
saltwort, spartina, distichlis spicata…
an exclusive neighborhood
at home in fresh or salt,
living in a world of its own
a buffer
a barrier
a solemn secluded edge,
dividing land and sea
salt and fresh.
It is at once neither
but ultimately both.

On the Pocomoke

Not all rivers divide continents
like the Mississippi.
The Pocomoke separates states,
Virginia and Maryland.
It is a river of restraint
a quiet black-water stream.

The Pocomoke has its wooded swamp,
a highway for migrating birds
like the prothonotary warbler,
a golden jewel
in the dark reaches of the swamp.

The lower Pocomoke runs deep and swift
joining the Chesapeake as a flooded ravine
pushed and pulled by the tides,
weekend boaters raising wakes
to rile the grasses on the shoreline.

But the upper Pocomoke
is dark and primal
cypress knees and old man's beard
black water flexing like steel.
Put in at Porter's Crossing
and after the first bend
you travel back....

no reminders of time or place,
just trees
black water flowing
reflecting trees and sky.

And then the spark of a golden bird
fittingly named for the prothonotarius,
the highest ranking of the papal clerks,
a bird that is God's accountant
and wears golden robes.

Hummocks

Hummocks are mysteries
written by the tides,
islands afloat in a sea of spartina.
Hummocks exist by inches,
a lifeline elevating them just enough
to grow pine, holly, cedars
and thickets of wax myrtle.
And so, on the horizon,
they make an emphatic statement.

Many years ago, the early settlers
pastured their livestock on hummocks,
and today they are mysteries
inaccessible to boats
unfriendly to foot travel.
From a distance,
you watch them in wonder
and curiosity,
could there be treasure there,
hidden by a pirate in a secret place
only he knew?

As the sea rises
hummocks are becoming ghost forests
the pines have dropped their greenery,
and are sharp silver relics
wasting away with each passing season.
In my child's time,
They will become spartina marshes,
just as fields that grew potatoes
in my father's time
have become marshland,
and today's upland forest
will be the hummock of tomorrow.

Thin Water Glide

The first moments in a small canoe
are like being weightless
floating in space
balanced on a fulcrum of water.

The less boat the better.
I have an Old Town Pack,
thirty-three pounds of Royalex
made to glide on thin water.
The pack takes me where there is too much water for walking
but not enough for boating.

At the head of Folly Creek I put in
where the racoons congregate,
their pungent remains scattered along the bank.
The canoe enters silently and glides
through tops of spartina grass,
sun burning into thin water
quivering like molten lead
in the wake.

There is not much water here
and there are no other people
no boats
just me and my little canoe
and we are not going far
just gliding through thin water
and drifting through space.

Sunrise and Ocean

In the moments before sunrise
the birds become alert
darting across a mauve sky
fragments from a waking dream.
They are like a crowd in a theatre
just before the curtain rises
twittering among themselves
muffling a call.

They are aloft and see the sun before we do
and make the announcement.
Gulls laugh and cry
coasting like puppets on strings.
Northern gannets pass in rough formation
soar and dip
fold wings and dive.

The sun is at half-mast
and the surf crashes like so many diamonds
scattering up the beach
then retreating to the sea.

A woman approaches with her phone
holds it at arms length
and I can see the sunrise on her screen.
She takes the picture, turns
and is quickly gone
capturing the treasure
to share with someone she loves.

Foodways

Clamming

We rake with picks
across dimples and puckers
littered with clam scat.
Then the metallic scrape
of steel on shell.
We dig and pry
and then it releases
relaxes
and is dislodged
with a healthy suck of mud.

It goes into the basket
with the others
soon to become
chowder or fritters
or perhaps some salty linguine,
pasta and clams
a marriage of sea and land.

Spot and Pigfish

Our granddaddies took their fish to market…
rockfish and flounder to be gutted and filleted
packed in ice
wrapped in plastic
and bagged for New Jersey tourists
heading home from the beach.

Our granddaddies brought home the spot and pigfish
for grandma to gut and scale
and fry in bacon drippings
shimmering like morning sun
in the black iron skillet on the stove.

Grandma left the heads and tails on
because the head sealed in that oily essence,
a shame to leave it in the pan,
and the tail gave up a crispy bite
unlike anything from a store.

I have nothing against rockfish and flounder,
they paid the rent and bought grandma's coffee,
and the clean white flesh is mild and flaky
no strong taste
isn't fishy.

But bring me
please
some spot and pigfish
with head and tail left on
hot from the pan and dripping bacon.

Fresh fish oil and bacon
and one fishy bite of tail.

Salted Fish

In the fall we would fish with purpose
not for trout to broil with wine and almonds,
but for spot and croaker
to fillet or butterfly
and pack away for winter
in stone crocks a century old....

a layer of salt
a layer of fish
and so it would go until the crock was filled
and capped with a tea towel and plate
taken to a dark corner of the pantry
and left to silently consummate a marriage,
salt and fish unite in a preserving brine.

It has been that way forever,
salt from the sea preserving fish of the sea
salt the original refrigeration
a chemical preservative that saved lives.

Without the salt of the sea
and the fish of the sea
the Jamestown colony would not have survived
would have become Virginia's Lost Colony.
And the mother tongue of coastal people
would not be English, but Spanish...or perhaps Dutch.

Fish of the Day

Parsnips, apples and dried cranberries
blended well with butter and cream
salmon seared on flesh and skin
then mushrooms, marsala, chard, and capers...

Sizzles and steams
like a summer storm
quickly passing
spent passion

Then salmon tops parsnips
and mushrooms thick glaze
glistens like honeydew
and glows on the platter
as though it had a light of its own.

Cock-a-leekie Soup

In a pub in the Yorkshire Dales
we had cock-a-leekie soup,
an unlikely wedding
of animal and plant...
the chicken's dark and soulful thigh
with smooth and elegant
stems of leek
green and white
tightly packed and firm
the chicken dark and sullen
the two joined together
by a handful of prunes
that perform this surprising ceremony
on a raw March walk
along the Pennine Way
in the very early days of Yorkshire spring.

Life on the Halfshell

Slurp that oyster from its shell
and let it rest upon your tongue
feel the cold and salty presence.

Can you feel the heart beat
on your tongue?

Seaside marsh in winter
taste of salt air
sky oyster gray and still,
the wild ripe saltmarsh fragrance
winter ritual of summer grasses
giving up their August heat,
sun they captured
now feeds the oyster
gives it winter life.

Can you taste this on your tongue?
life so salt and wild
a brine that speaks of time and place.

Close your eyes
bite gently into cold gray flesh
taste the salty winter cascade.

Close your eyes
it will take you there.

Bessie Gunter

Feeding the family was a brutal sport
in the days of Bessie Gunter.
Bessie wrote a cookbook for the church building fund
and filled it with violence and mayhem.

To cook a terrapin
she advised
plunge it head first into boiling water
this will kill it instantly
remove from the feet the skin and nails
remove the head and tail
and take the gall from the liver
being careful not to squeeze.

Bessie was no doubt a good Baptist
a kind and gentle creature
who had no idea providing for her family
was involving acts of violence.

It was how things were done.
God's way of providing for his children
like rail hunting and hog killing
a ceremony of death to sustain life.

The ceremony today is seldom seen,
hidden beneath the layers of consumerism.
Food is no longer part of the cycle of life,
but a product of industry.
Sausage does not come from family hog killings,
but is made by a company in China
named for a dead country music singer,
packaged in plastic tubes
as if it involved no living thing.

We are reminded
traveling the highways
trailing a truck with chickens
packed tightly in coops
stacked in neat rows
white feathered marsh hens
heading to a place never seen
to be packed in styrofoam trays
and advertised in the weekly circular
a dollar ninety-nine a pound.

Clam Chowder

The clam exists for two reasons,
to eat and to have sex,
hence the saying
happy as a clam.

In spring
when the thermometer hits the erogenous zone
the brother and sister clams
cloud the water with eggs and semen
a protein broth that joins the plankton
feeding the creatures of the estuary.

The clam feeds me as well
and it has fed many who came before,
those who came with stone tools
prying the clam from its muddy home
roasting it over fire
and suckling its sweet salty meat.

And nothing has changed
since those stone-tool people prowled the flats.
I find a dimple in the wet mud
scratch through it with my metal pick
and pry the clam loose and take it home.

I make a broth of my clams,
potatoes and onions I grew,
and I taste the seaside
sweet and salty
the essence of my home.

Love Dumplings

He buried her more than a year ago
but each night he prepares her dinner.
On Sundays chicken and dumplings
made with her favorite biscuits.
He sets a place for her and sits opposite
quietly and slowly, as if in a dream,
having his dinner.

His son asked him why
after all this time.
And he said that preparing food for someone
is the purest way to tell them you love them.
Although she no longer is at the table,
he needs to tell her she is loved.

Grandma's Hog's Jole

It is a shame farmers don't have hog killings anymore.
we have lost an entire food lexicon....
souse and sidemeat and chitterlins have left the stage
sausage was made on the kitchen table
ground by hand and mixed with pepper and sage
stuffed into the hog's own intestine,
a twisted chain of links
hung from the porch ceiling all winter.

My grandmother's favorite pork part was hog's jole
the jowl of the hog, fatty and tender,
but she didn't pronounce it jowl
she gave it a long "o" sound
a deliciously alliterative phrase
hog's jole.

Grandma taught Sunday School for forty years
and when she spoke of hog's jole
she did so with the reverence shown Sunday communion
or the Woman's Christian Temperance Union.
Grandma said she used hog's jole for seasoning greens
but she was known to crisp some with the eggs.

We were in Washington one summer
and had lunch at a fancy French restaurant.
The salad included lardons,
which I had never had before,
but with one salty bite I knew it at once...
Grandma's hog's jole in the nation's capital
senators and congressmen
lobbyists and lawyers
the rich and the famous
and we were all eating Grandma's hog jole.

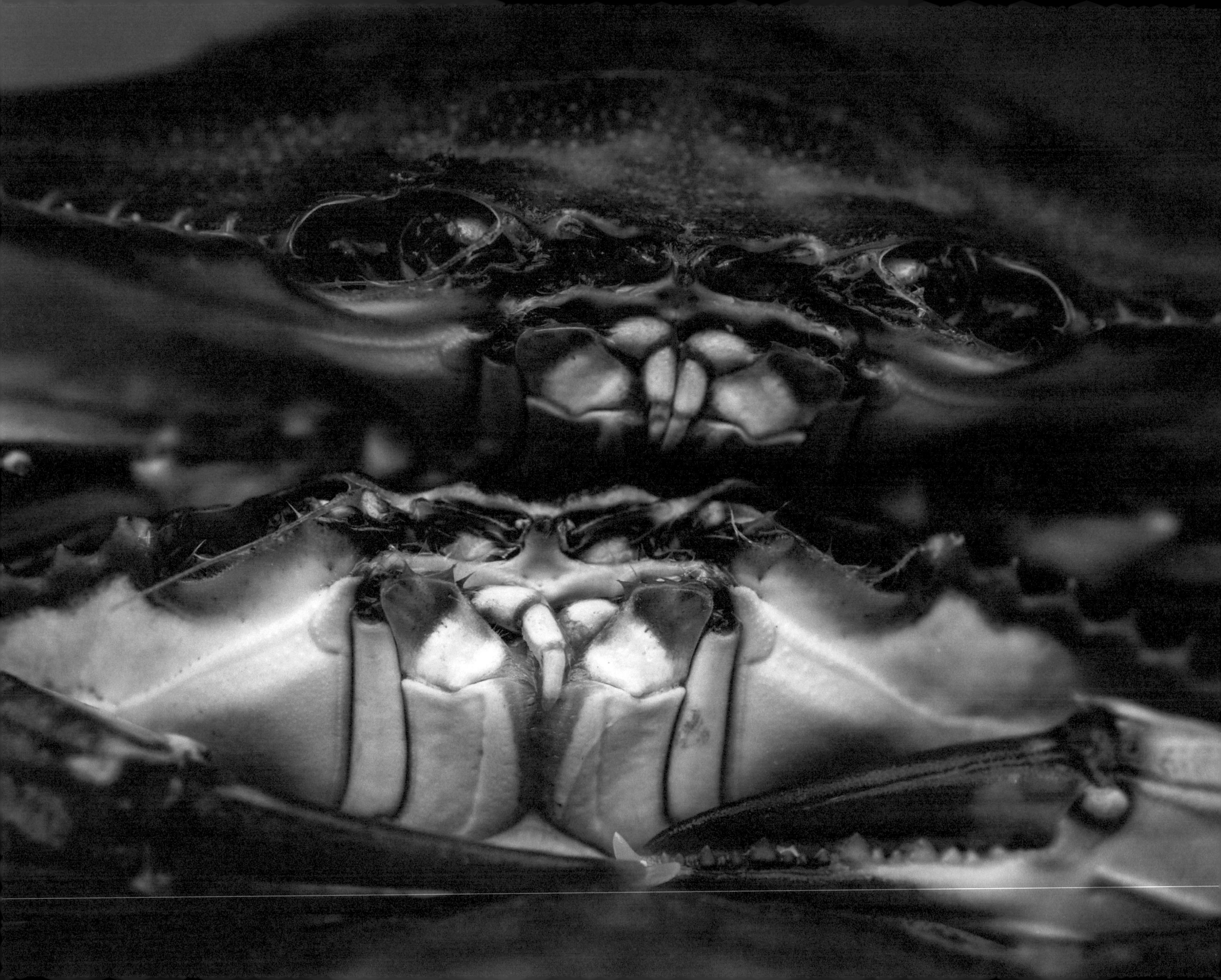

The Women All Singing
(Eastern Shore Seafood, Bayside, summer 1972)

The women gather around steel tables
with crab knives and thick aprons
and the steaming pot releases its load
blue crabs
red now
after thirty minutes cooking
scattered along the table
beneath a fragrant cloud of steam.

A man with heavy black gloves
shoves the crabs like broken toys
from one end to the other
as the women stop their talk
and take their places.

Soon the room is silent
save the click and crack of crab shell
back shell pried away
revealing sweet lump below.

And soon a rhythm begins
as crab meat fills the plastic tubs
and a woman begins to hum
some old time gospel song
and another joins in

and then another
and the room is working to the rhythm
of an old Sunday hymn
known from childhood,
and the women sing together
in reverent harmony
And soon the tubs are filled
with lump, claw, and backfin....
praise his precious name.

Digging Potatoes

I plant potatoes on my birthday
March 27
It seems a proper celebration of birth.
Yukon Gold and redskins from Maine
go into our raised beds
worked until the soil is light and forgiving
willing to welcome growing sprouts.
Seed potatoes have eyes, beginning to wink,
fresh green growth of this year's crop.

By June the new plants blossom
white flowers on the Yukons
blue on the redskins.
And when the blossoms fade
I begin my search
grabbling with my fingers in the soil
finding firm globes tethered by a plant umbilical
nurturing this new life.

The new potatoes are delicate
unlike anything in a store.
You could peel them with your thumb
if you wanted to.
But they are rinsed gently
and boiled for ten minutes
no more…
and then laced with butter and sea salt
and eaten with fresh peas
that grew in the row next door.

Apple Pie

My father liked his apple pie
warm and topped with sharp cheddar.
I like apples cold and chunky
with a dusting of blue cheese crumbles.
Granny Smith firm and tangy
blue cheese earth and salty
a sprinkle of dried mint
doesn't hurt either.

In November I eat a slice of pie and cheddar
in honor of his birthday.
The apples are warm and sweet
cinnamon and crusty
the cheese orange and assertive
the kind they cut from a big wheel
wrapped in moldy cloth
in a store with warped wooden floors
that burned many years ago.

Closer to Home

The Birth of the Day

We sit in silence and watch the birth of the day
light moving silently
like a fox through the forest
turning trees to shadows,
and beyond the shadows
the creek flowing like a silver ribbon
heralding the birth of the day.

We silently sip our coffee
as we watch the sky
and an eagle appears black on gray
pitches in the top of a loblolly pine
eagle you say.

We share our silence like a sumptuous feast
to be enjoyed at leisure
plates taken one at a time
no need to rush I say.

The silence we share is precious
a gift we quietly treasure
knowing that one of us
someday
will sit here silent
and alone
watching the birth of the day.

The Cat

Lying on her back before the fire

the cat yawns and looks at me with half-open eyes

she looks sleep drunk

forepaws drawn to her chest

legs splayed

white belly seam stretching through the gray

to a silken primordial pouch

with a touch of orange.

You are such a slut I tell her

she whips her tail back and forth

thump thump against the floor

I am tempted to give her a belly rub

but I know what she is thinking….

she will bite me if I do.

Brant

The brant is the wild goose of the seaside
a wintertime visitor
seldom seen
by flounder fishermen and clammers
beachcombers and sunbathers.

The brant travels in ragged flocks
not the famous V-formation of the Canadas.
The brant is dark,
black head and breast
flanks gray-brown and mottled
the rump white.

The brant looks right in the marsh in winter,
flanks the color of decaying spartina
breast and neck the daub mud of the flat
white rump a chunk of salt ice
scoured from an oyster rock by a hard freeze
cast away on a rising tide.

The brant's call is wild
high-pitched and feminine,
hesitant
as if afraid to interrupt,
a wilder version of the Canada
whose stock has become diminished,
no longer wild and too familiar
now the bird of the golf course
the green lawns of chicken plants
the sidewalks of the office park.

It deposits its green pellets to soil the shoes
of the accountant's clients.

The brant is the wild goose no one knows.

Jimmy King

In the air force my roommate was Jimmy King.
I had never lived with a black man before
and I'm sure he had never lived with a white.
We were awkwardly courteous.

Jimmy grew up on a farm in rural Georgia.
My family were farmers in Virginia…
big families
aunts, uncles, cousins, grandparents.
We ate from the garden in summer
had hog killing in the winter.
Jimmy and I spoke of cured hams
country bacon, scrapple and hog's jowl.

By the end of a week
we were like peas in a pod
a white pea and a brown pea
but peas just the same.

People share this earth
without knowing each other
pushed apart by unseen forces
like poles on a magnet
separate but equal they said
knowing it was neither.

We were born into the same world
yet separated by something we cannot comprehend
like a wound unable to heal
we stood side by side
talked but did not communicate
took but did not give
looked but did not see.

I was going to the PO one day and asked Jimmy if he
had anything to mail.
He handed me a letter
addressed to his cousin in Melfa, Virginia
my home town.

Clinging to the Bough

I once cared for the old
and now I am the old.
I shall wear the bottoms of my trousers rolled,
said the poet.

But what does that mean,
what does it mean to grow old?
Do we leave our home where we raised a family
to move into a more modest place
a bungalow with an upstairs guest room
and an eat-in kitchen,
or a room at the retirement home
where breakfast is served on a plastic tray
and relatives reluctantly visit
out of duty
out of expectation of what may be coming their way?

What about the sunrise as the creek awakens,
the deer that tip-toe carefully across the yard
like shy visitors who come to call?
What about the wood ducks on the pond in winter,
the green herons that gather in summer
building nests in the wax myrtles?
What about the memories of clearing land
building a home
training the high bush blueberries to increase their yield?

What about the neighbors who have become as family?
What about the things that fill the house
made by people we know so well?

We hang on like a fall season
edging toward winter
like the leaves on the beech tree
that wither and fade
yet cling steadfastly to the bough
certain they will last forever.

MRI

I am in the MRI scanner
and it is banging out
live images of cysts and ganglia
worming their way
like invasive amoebae
among the vertebrae in my spine.

When the banging ceases
I breathe deep and think
of the ocean.
I can hear my heart....
not a beat but a flush,
the movement of fluid,
squeeze, push, vacate
repeat.

I think of surf breaking
rolling like a liquid seam,
rolling up the berm
a green moving cylinder of water
spinning off silver spray
and finally collapsing
into a lace of white foam
that withers and sinks
like a lost thought
into sand.

I am on my back
eyes closed
and the scanner begins again
hammering
hammering
and I think of the ocean
and keep my eyes closed.
Afraid to see something
that has become
uncomfortably near.

The Cat, 2

Maggie is a biter.
Maggie was a dumpster kitty
hunkered under a trash bin when we found her
matted gray striped fur
just bones and fur
a kitten someone did not want
and took to the landfill for disposal.

So Maggie is a biter
without meaning to be.
The quick movement of a hand
provokes her to strike.
It surprises her when it happens
and she looks shocked and frightened
puzzled and embarrassed
by her reflexive act of violence.
She apologizes profusely.

Maggie is a beautiful cat
gray stripes arranged symmetrically along her back and flanks,
white chin and affluent underbelly with a hint of orange....
you would never know Maggie came from a dumpster
considered garbage by a cruel person
who painfully taught her
to fear the human hand.

Radio People

Some people are like a radio
turned up a bit too loud
and you don't really care
what the radio is saying
but it would be rude
to turn it down
or to unplug it
because the radio is
deriving great pleasure
from the sound it makes.
It is clever,
it is funny,
it is entertaining.
So you let the radio play
because it gives the radio pleasure
and it makes you realize
what a beautiful sound it is
when the radio goes away
and the silence returns.

The Cat and the Clock

Each week I wind the family clock
which once graced my grandmother's mantel.
The cat leaps onto the sideboard
the moment I begin to wind....
She nudges my arm as I twist the key
rubs the glass door in intense pleasure
as the spring tightens with a mechanical purr
the key turns in a rhythm like breathing
pulsing and purring as I wind
until at last the spring tightens
and the cat nuzzles the clock a final time....
and dreams of next week
when we wind another time.

Spoiling the Cat

Someone told us today we are spoiling our cat.
We have made every attempt to do so,
but whether we have succeeded is unknown,
spoiling a cat is a work in progress.

Our cat was dropped off at the county dump.
Her first weeks hunkered
under a metal dumpster.
She panicked every few days
when a truck backed up to the dumpster,
its reverse alarm beeping,
and when the beeping stopped
her home was whisked away
like a tent in a tornado.

And today, two years later,
she panics when the gas truck
backs into the driveway
beep, beep, beep, beep
louder as it approaches the house.
She makes a guttural cry of primal fear
races around the house
finally hides under the bed.
And when the beeping stops
she cautiously emerges,
eyes wild and darting.

And so we try to spoil her,
and if we spoil her for the rest of her life,
it might take twenty years
for her life to come out even.

And perhaps this should apply
to people as well.
Some of us are born to solid families
and some begin life
hunkered under dumpsters
through no fault of their own.
We cannot choose our parents.

Perhaps these, too, need spoiling
that is…
loved, valued, nourished, cared for, treated with kindness…
to make their lives come out even.

The Concrete Fleet

They rest at ease
on the sandy bottom of Kiptopeke Landing
where they once protected
a busy harbor
where ferries steamed across the capes
linking the Eastern Shore and Little Creek.

They are a fleet of nine
linked end to end
bow to stern
navy veterans made of concrete
served in the last World War.
And now they are gray ghosts
weathered to reveal a pallet of colors
hulking like a parade of monoliths
at the mouth of the bay.

They have performed their job well.
The old harbor
protected by these concrete barriers
has held steadfast since 1949.
The shoreline north and south
has migrated east, but the pier has held its ground
behind this protective line.

The concrete fleet, the flotilla of nine,
was towed here after the war,
lashed together and scuttled,
settled in the sand of Kiptopeke Beach
protecting the dockage of ferries
until the ferries no longer sailed.

And now they are a curiosity,
a concrete fleet
protecting a fishing pier.
Now part of the landscape
no longer ships that once sailed with soldiers.

Now they are history
duty done
ships made of sand and cement
slowly returning to the world
from which they came.

Fatwood Fire Starter

In the short days of winter
when the wind rakes the stubble in the soybean field
we search for fatwood
in the gentle shelter of the forest.

In stumps left from pines
harvested when our parents were young
a vein remains that once connected trunk to root.

The pulp has long since rotted
leaving a ragged arm of resin
sap a century old
revealed when the pulp fell away.

It smells of turpentine
the essence of pine
waiting quietly to be discovered
given a new purpose
nature's fire starter.

Honeysuckle Always Climbs Clockwise

Honeysuckle always climbs clockwise
never the other way around.
Around the trunk of a sassafras sapling
climbing as it follows the sun
it wraps the sassafras so tightly
the two become as one.

As seasons pass the vine wraps tighter
becoming part of the tree.
A sassafras snake climbing,
like hands on the clock
up and up
tighter and tighter…
Until it becomes no longer a vine
and no longer a tree
but something entirely new.

I cut the sapling and let it dry
then carefully peel the bark away,
polish it with linseed oil
and there appears a walking stick
with a honeysuckle snake
forever climbing clockwise.

Wisteria

In spring its purple blossoms
invade the pine woods
desperate for light,
like strands of DNA
reaching back generations
when my people lived here.

Wisteria is all that remains
of the homeplace and the barns
the peach orchard and grapes
the grave of someone who died at sea
and was brought to this corner of the field
and laid to rest.

Wisteria blooms in May
and winds its tangled way
through the tree tops
leaving its message
that all the things we thought lasting
are not.

It blooms just once to remind us
and then it fades and multiplies
and next year it will remind us again.
And again we will remember.

Gifts of Time and Place

The time came
when we stopped giving things for Christmas,
no more sweaters and ties
the scarves and ear rings were history
instead, we exchanged gifts of time and place.

For her
two nights in Rehoboth Beach
at our favorite hotel
ceviche and patos with olives
at Mariachi
with margaritas.

By day
Bombay Hook with snow geese
ballet and symphony in one
they pass in animated clouds
announcing their arrival in song
then settle among the stubble of corn....
some wear yellow collars
given on birthing grounds in Arctic tundra.

For him
two nights at the Outer Banks
oysters at Darrel's
fried with a delicate hand
oysters on the half-shell
with a crust
seaside slurp with a crisp.

By day
Alligator River and Bodie Island
Pea Island and the pintails
tundra swans and avocets
and gannets diving beyond the breakers,
a cold wind from the ocean.

We leave the sliding door open
just a crack
to sleep to the perfect rhythm
the crash and roar
hiss of retreat
and the gift of sunrise in the morning.

Lake Floyd

Mighty Lake Floyd is the size of a football field
but appears smaller
because the black locusts and wax myrtles
have reduced its margins
leaning over its slack water
thirsty for light....
some appear to be growing from the water itself.

The lake was created by Floyd Nock
an architect and friend who designed the community we live in.
Lake Floyd's purpose was to hold rainwater
that washed from the yards and streets
and to gradually return it to Pungoteague Creek
and the Chesapeake Bay in a cleaner state.

Lake Floyd is a stormwater retention pond,
a cold and sterile engineering term that
leaves no hint of the variety of life the lake supports.
So prolific is the lake we knew it needed a name
and so we named it for Floyd.

Lake Floyd provides testimony of what nature can do
if you just leave it alone.
Turn your back to it, ignore it and let it live in peace.
It will do fine without you.
So the wax myrtles grow dense
and the locust trees reach for light like basketball players
leaping for a rebound.

Ferns grow wild around the edges
and blueberries grow on the berm
propagated by robins and jays.
In October the wood ducks arrive
and stay until May
some nest in tree cavities and raise a brood.

Summer is the time of green herons
nesting in the wax myrtles
fishing in the pond
and along the stream that feeds it.
Small fish have appeared as if by magic
dropping from the heavens.
Bullfrogs grumble and bellow on summer mornings
Red-bellied turtles lumber out of the water
and search for sand to lay eggs.
Dragonflies hover and cast their shadows on black water
touch their abdomen to release eggs.
Water snakes sun on the trunks of fallen gums
one eye open as they slumber
in case a tadpole should pass.

Lake Floyd flourishes upon neglect....
no humans to decide which plant lives
and which plant dies
and that snakes must die
because they are snakes
and that some plants must be eliminated
because they make humans break out in a rash.

The Ebb and Flood of Birds

On May 13 the green heron arrives
followed shortly by a hummingbird,
both right on time.
In the seaside marshes whimbrels fly
in ragged flocks
chasing the edge of tides and looking for water.
They fly with an urgent hunger
having completed a trip of a thousand miles
from marshland in Cuba,
and now they settle on tidal flats
beyond the water's reach
and probe the burrows of fiddler crabs
with curved beaks.

On beaches the oystercatchers gather
with terns and plovers and black skimmers
whose red beaks cut through quiet waters
dipping to snag a small fish.

A squadron of dunlin fly in precise formation
wing tip to wing tip,
sweep over the flats in a choreographed dance
like a school of menhaden
when the tide is high and rising.

A great blue heron settles sedately
on a tidal drain that cuts through marsh.
The heron is heading home to Maine to nest once again
in a flooded forest outside Bangor.
Last September the heron flew from Bangor
to Bermuda non-stop,
and the next day to the Bahamas
and then to a marsh on the south shore
of Cuba near Guantanamo,
spending her winter there.
Her return trip is a leisure voyage,
visiting the islands and waterways of Virginia
making her way up the coast
drawn by an innate need to move.

The ebb and flood push her
as surely as it pushes water.

Too Late to Die Young

When I was a child I knew I would die young
in a war
in a desert
amid dry and parched earth
where the wind blew sand to disguise the enemy.
It was a dream that came regularly
not with fear
but with complacency.
It was a given.

But my dream was wrong
and now it is too late for me to die young.
I joined the air force
and my weapon was a Nikon
my ammo was Tri-X
in 36-exposure rolls.
I shot my way from Brazil to Alaska
taking no prisoners
capturing only moments in time
at 1/250th at f/8.
And now I am too late to die young
and too young to die.

Passion, Not Money

The passage of birth
brings with it a death sentence.
All you are guaranteed
are the beginning and the end.
What happens in between
is up to you.

The goal of life is to find your passion.
Your life is going to be short,
what do you want to do with it?
Don't worry about money,
unless money is your passion.
But do what gives you pleasure and satisfaction.
If it is building things,
then build things.
If it is healing people,
then heal people.
If it is law,
then follow the law.

Just follow your passion,
and not money.
If you follow your passion
and you pursue it fully,
money will follow
without being sought.
And if you bought this little book,
thank you very much.

1/250 at f/8

Capturing time and making it your own

at 1/250 at f/8.

A moment fleeting is frozen

like a rare bird

shot by a 19th century naturalist,

taking a life to study it.

A moment is transformed

from time to history

caught in a pose it will forever hold.

And what do we make of it?

A fraction of a second of forever

and when the shutter clicks

it is transformed from present to past.

Time has become matter.

A thought or a breath

or a word once said

seized by the shutter

at 1/250 at f/8

and given eternal life.

The Day the Old Hotel Burned

Saturday morning
in my mother's kitchen,
yeast rolls rising
and a hot iron
pressing damp cloth
on the ironing board.
A humid cloud,
steam sweetly rising
on a hot Saturday morning.

A cake is in the oven
and she warns me
not to let the screen door slam,
or the cake
just risen
will fall.

A cake so sensitive to sound
it will collapse
with the careless shutting of a door.

The radio
and the morning hymns
the news
and Arthur Godfrey.

And then the morning
when we smelled smoke
and went outside
to see flames from the old hotel,
set afire by sparks from a passing train.

We heard the sirens and bells
throughout the day,
and in the evening
the pall of wood smoke
huddled over the town
like wet burlap simmering.

Blind old Charlie McCready,
they said,
was found in his second-floor room....
an empty bottle of Ancient Age
on the table by his bed.

Family Matters

The Red Bank Place

Captain Tom in his prime
had sixty acres on Red Bank Creek
a schooner moored nearby
and a peach orchard that yielded fine brandy.
Captain Tom owned fifteen slaves
to provide the horsepower to drive his enterprise.

The census numbers are cold and without judgement.
He owned one bull, three cows, hogs and chickens
a plow and mule
and depending upon the season,
eight to fifteen Negroes.
Owned them.

The census presents like the result of a biopsy.
The shock like ice and disbelief
you feel it deep and cold in your gut
and slowly it warms and you tell yourself
that's just the way it was.
You can't exorcise it, so deal with it.
That's the way it was.

Captain Tom was no plantation owner.
He had a mule and a plow and he needed help,
someone to walk with him
and drop seed potatoes into the furrow
someone to help harvest peaches
grind the corn, cut the firewood, mend the fences.

These were the days before people worked for money.
Some were indentured and worked for room and
board
a chance to learn a skill
others were tenants
providing labor for a share
if there was one.
And some were owned
fed and clothed
worked like a tool
and passed along
to an owner not of their choosing.

Captain John

Captain John
not long before his death
posed for a picture on his porch
in a suit seldom worn
except at Thanksgiving
when the family gathered for a last time
and the photographer snapped the shutter.

"We are nearly all here,"
someone wrote in the margin of the print.
Captain John is lean like fatwood in his tweed suit
the pulp worn away to reveal the essence of his core.
He sits in his rocker
slim legs crossed
and family gather around him
smiling.

Genetic Navigation

I walk in the woods before dawn
dodging shadows and thickets of greenbrier.
My grandfather walked here
and his father before him
in the woods of Red Bank Farm
down to the creek beyond the woods
down to where the black ducks fly.

I need no light to guide me.
I know the way through shadows and vines.
It was passed along to me
just as birds know in their first year
the route they must take....
Genetic navigation.

I walk the path to the shore at dawn
reaching my cedar blind before light.
In the east the sky glows,
in the air the whistle of wings
shadows flash black across the sky.

I set the decoys and hide and wait
listen amid quiet for the rush of wings
then the touch of birds on still water.
My grandfather hears them too.

Aunt Easter

Aunt Easter was born in 1825 to one of Captain Tom's slaves,
and at an early age her job was to care for and protect Tom's
son John.
She cared for John from the time of his birth until he died.
After his death she cared for his widow and children and
took the family name.

John left the farm with his older brother in 1849
to go to the Gold Rush in California
and when he left, he gave Easter her freedom
but when he returned ten years later
she returned to the farm to be with him.
She cooked meals in the fireplace
and loved John as a son.
On court days she would go to Eastville
and cook at the Eastville Inn.

John's daughter Margaret, in a memoir, wrote
"Easter always had a cup of hot coffee for John when he
awoke in the morning.
Sometimes I would read to her.
At night when her legs hurt
I would rub them in hot vinegar.
In her last days, Mama and I nursed her
until she passed away.

She loved me better than she loved anyone
except Marse John
and I loved her
as I loved my own family."

In a photograph taken in 1901
Aunt Easter sits with
John and his wife Sue and all the family
gathered on the front porch.
She sits on the steps
away from the others,
and while they look toward the camera and smile
Aunt Easter looks aside
and seems to be searching for something in the distance.

I Am Not the Child You Lost

I am not the child you lost
I am the child who came much later.
Your child left before I came.
She was the family story.

It was an accident, the paper said
a fall while playing on a tricycle
not polio or meningitis as other parents feared.

Most of the town came to view her
at rest in a small pink coffin
in the front room, amid a sea of rose petals.
They passed by slowly, reverently
some looked into her closed eyes
some averted eyes
and some wept.

You sat in the corner and cried softly
as if some part of you had left the room
never to return.
You were comforted by her father
my father.

The child you lost was an angel
a neighbor told me.
God had taken her back to Heaven
to be with other angels.

When the angel left, she took something of you with her
and replaced it with an emptiness you could not fill.
I could not fill
nor would you let me.
I could not become the child you lost.

You tried
but there was always the darkness
the words you hurled as weapons
intended to inflict pain.

Are you trying to kill us, your father and me?
I had missed my 11 p.m. curfew by 15 minutes.

Are you proud of yourself, the way you turned out?
I don't know. I probably flunked algebra.

I am the child who came much later
but I was not the angel you wanted.
The angel left before I came.
Perhaps the child you lost
was the wrong child.

Some Wounds Do Not Bleed

Some wounds do not bleed
and some wounds do not heal.
Maggie was abused as a kitten
dumped in a landfill like garbage.
Although she is a fat cat now
her wounds have never healed.

Sometimes she bites
not out of aggression
but as an act of defense
establishing limits
she learned as a kitten
when being abused.

People also have wounds that do not bleed
invisible wounds that never heal.
My mother lost her two-year-old child
in an accident.

She began her day with a beautiful daughter
with curly blonde hair and a dazzling smile.
She ended her day in mourning
childless.

I never contemplated the depth of this trauma
until I became a father
and then I felt the cold blade as it sliced into her heart.

But she never bled, did she?
she never bled
and there might have been times
when she wished the blade had brought the end.

My mother's life was changed over the space of one day
as if she had been blinded by lightning
or struck by a car and left paralyzed.
But she wasn't blinded, wasn't paralyzed
and she wore no wound for the world to see.

No one would pass her on the sidewalk and remark
how sad
how terribly, terribly sad that she was chosen to endure
this.

And like Maggie, my mother lashed out
built a wall
created a dark side
a necessary invention.

Building a wall to hide a wound
was an act of defense, not aggression.
It put her in a safe place
where she would never feel the cold sudden blade another
time.

A Christmas Story

Christmas was the season
spent with my grandmother
whose large house welcomed children and grandchildren
aunts and uncles.

My mother preferred to have Christmas in her own home
with just our family.
So the holiday pilgrimage to grandmother's house
was a journey darkened by resentment,
although the journey involved a walk of five minutes
from our house to hers
it was a doleful march.

My mother's resentment, her simmering anger
was part of her Christmas tradition
and she wore it like a holiday sweater
frazzled and old
and not unexpected.

My grandmother ignored the resentment,
the frazzled sweater
and transported herself to an earlier time
when as a child her family gathered
not just for a Christmas dinner
but for days at Big Momma and Big Papa's farm.

The gathering came at the close of hog killing time,
the annual ritual when family and friends
would rise before dawn
and by nightfall have the smokehouse
stocked with hams and bacon
shoulders and scrapple
and dozens of sausage links
made from spiced pork stuffed into hog intestine,
draped like fragrant ornaments from the rafters.

The Christmas my mother resented
was a reenactment of Christmas past for my grandmother,
who summoned family and friends
for a ritual none of them had known,
but they played the part and delivered their lines
like the Christmas pageant in church.

My grandmother was a widow
and enjoyed the annual connection with family
and friends
of having the big house filled with the play of children
the laughter of adults
if only for a day.

I suspect
for some reason
my mother would have gained satisfaction
denying her that.

My grandmother had a modern kitchen
but she kept a wood-burning cookstove in the cellar
and Christmas meant many trips down the cellar
where the country ham and yeast rolls
the turkey and oyster dressing
would simmer and brown
and the warm aroma of cherry wood and ham
would rise and press against the low ceiling
hanging there in a fragrant mist
until someone opened the cellar door
and it would rush down the hallway to the dining room
announcing its great promise....

And then we all would gather,
the adults at the big table
the children at theirs
the adults beginning the feast with raw oysters
and vague jokes about libido
the children did not understand.
Eat fish live longer,
Eat oysters love longer.

And so there was laughter
and for a time
we were all living
in the same moment
not an era of my grandmother's past
not a dark hour of my mother's resentment.
The cellar door had opened
and light had filled the room.

I think I heard my mother smile.

The Red Tricycle

I found a red tricycle in my grandmother's barn
behind bushel baskets that once held potatoes.

Draped with dusty sacks of burlap,
the chrome handlebars
were cratered with rust
and bent at an odd angle.

I pulled away the burlap
and pushed aside the baskets
and as I reached for the handlebars
my grandmother touched my shoulder.

That is not something you should be playing with, she said.
I left the tricycle and walked with my grandmother to the house
silently.

Two days later, the tricycle was gone
only the baskets and burlap remained
nothing else was said....

Other Books by Curtis J. Badger

Salt Tide — Cycles and Currents of Life Along the Coast

Bellevue Farm — Exploring Virginia's Coastal Countryside

The Wild Coast — Swamps and Wetlands of the Mid-Atlantic Coast

Virginia's Wild Side — 50 Outdoor Adventures from the Mountains to the Ocean

A Natural History of Quiet Waters

Exploring Delmarva

A Culinary History of Delmarva

Wilderness Regained — The Story of the Virginia Barrier Islands

Peninsulas in Repose — The Necks of Virginia's Eastern Shore

Books for Young Readers:

Nathan Cobb's Island

Hog Island

Assateague — The Island of Ponies

Birds of the Barrier Islands